SCORCH

by Stacey Gregg

Scorch was first performed at the Outburst
Queer Arts Festival, Belfast, in 2015.

It was presented in Paines Plough's Roundabout at the
2016 Edinburgh Festival Fringe, before touring Ireland.

SCORCH

by Stacey Gregg

THE COMPANY

KESSY   Amy McAllister

Director   Emma Jordan
Set & Lighting Design   Ciaran Bagnall
Sound Design   Carl Kennedy
Costume Design   Enda Kenny
Movement Director   Nicola Curry
Movement Consultant   Oona Dorherty
Video/Filming   Conn McKermott
Production Manager   Ross McDade
Stage Manager   Ashley Smyth
Graphic Design   Ben Willis at HiJump
Producer   Una NicEoin

Prime Cut would also like to thank the following people and organisations:

Ruth McCarthy, Alice Kennelly, Cian Smith and all the team at Outburst Queer Arts Festival; Gilly Campbell and Debbie Young at Arts Council NI; Naomi Doak and Eimear Henry at Belfast City Council; Ushi Bagga at Paul Hamlyn Foundation; all the team at The MAC, Belfast; Kate Danielson and the Weston Jerwood Foundation; Clare Shepherd; Giles Smart; Sammy Kate Smith; Tania Carlisle, Brona Whittaker and all the team at Arts & Business NI; Roise Goan; Ruth Little; Jason Ashford; Matt Curry; James Copeland; Robin Renwick.

BIOGRAPHIES

Amy McAllister – Kessy

Theatre credits include: *Forever Yours Mary-Lou* (Theatre Royal Bath); *Hecuba* (Royal Shakespeare Company); *The Shadow of a Gunman* (Abbey/Lyric); *Sons Without Fathers* (Arcola/Belgrade); *White Rabbit, Red Rabbit* (Live Theatre); *Too Small to Be a Planet, Holes* (Company of Angels/Latitude); *Horse Piss For Blood* (Plymouth Drum); *No Man's Land* (West Yorkshire Playhouse/Theater an der Parkaue); *Brighton Beach Memoirs* (Watford Palace); *His Dark Materials* (Birmingham Rep/West Yorkshire Playhouse); *The Lion, the Witch and the Wardrobe* (Royal Lyceum); *The Lady from the Sea* (Birmingham Rep); *Don Juan Comes Back From the War* (Belgrade); *The Tinker's Wedding, Playgoers, Nan* (Orange Tree); *Little Mermaid* (Polka/York Theatre Royal); *The Way Home* (Liverpool Everyman); *Live Like Pigs* (Royal Court/GSMD).

Television credits include: *The Great Fire, Emmerdale* (ITV); *Call the Midwife, Holby City, Doctors* (BBC); *Raymond* (TV Loonland); *Nearly Famous* (Channel4/E4).

Film credits include: *Philomena, Ruby Strangelove, Angel.*

Radio credits include: *The Van, The Snapper* (BBC).

Amy is also a former UK-Anti-Slam Champion.

Stacey Gregg – Playwright

Stacey Gregg is from Belfast and is a writer and performer for stage and screen. Previous work includes *Perve* (BBC Radio Drama Award 2012) and *Shibboleth* (Abbey, Dublin); *Lagan* (Ovalhouse, London); *Override* (Watford Palace); *Huzzies* (Tinderbox, The Mac); National Theatre Connections, and as a performer *Moth* (Bush/HighTide); *Pussy Riot* (Bush/Southbank Centre) and *Everything Between Us* (Rough Magic). Stacey is currently under commission with the Royal Exchange Theatre, Manchester. She created an interactive web installation for CRASSH (Centre For Research in the Arts, Social Sciences and Humanities), a sound installation *Thunderhead* (Royal Court), and was resident at Clean Break, working with women in the criminal justice system. Television work includes *Spoof or Die* (Channel4), *The Frankenstein Chronicles* and *Riviera*. She is a MacDowell fellow.

Emma Jordan – Director
Emma is Prime Cut's Artistic Director and her directing credits for the company include: Willy Russell's *Educating Rita* (2016), Patrick Marber's *After Miss Julie* (2016), Stacey Gregg's *Scorch* (2015), Yasmina Reza's *The God of Carnage* (2015), *The Conquest of Happiness* for Derry-Londonderry City of Culture and European tour (2013), Doug Wright's *I Am My Own Wife* (2012), David Harrower's *Blackbird* (2011), Owen McCafferty's *Shoot the Crow* (2011 & 2012), Fiona Evans's *Scarborough* (2010), Marina Carr's *Woman and Scarecrow* (2009), Dennis Kelly's *After the End* (2008), and a staged reading of Fermin Cabal's *Tejas Verdes* (Old Museum Arts Centre). Emma's acting credits include work with numerous theatre companies including: Charabanc, Tinderbox, the Lyric Theatre, Replay, Dubblejoint and Young at Art. Her producing credits for Prime Cut include *Three Tall Women* (Assistant Director), *The Coronation Voyage*, *Shopping and Fucking*, *American Buffalo*, *Macbeth*, *The Chance*, *After Darwin*, *The Mercy Seat*, *Ashes to Ashes*, *A Number*, *Cold Comfort*, *The Trestle at Pope Lick Creek*, *Scenes From the Big Picture*, Owen McCafferty's version of *Antigone*, *Vincent River*, *The Chilean Trilogy*, and most recently Jack Thorne's *Mydidae*.

In 2014 Emma was the recipient of the Paul Hamlyn Cultural Entrepreneurship Breakthrough Award and in 2015 the Spirit of Festival Award at the Belfast International Arts Festival.

Ciaran Bagnall – Set & Lighting Design
Ciaran is an Artistic Associate of Prime Cut Productions. He trained at the Welsh College of Music and Drama in Cardiff. Designs for Prime Cut include set and lighting design for *The God of Carnage*, *Tejas Verdes*, *Villa*, *Discurso*, *The Conquest of Happiness*, *I Am My Own Wife*, *The Baths*, *Shoot the Crow*, *Scarborough*, *Woman and Scarecrow*, *Still Life Still* and lighting design on *Mydidae*, *Right here, Right now*, *Antigone* and *After the End*.

Recent set and lighting designs: *The Train* (Rough Magic); *Othello* (Royal Shakespeare Company); *Lally the Scut* (MAC, Belfast); *A View from the Bridge*, *Love Story*, *Twelfth Night*, *Piaf*, *Of Mice and Men*, *Tull*, *The Glass Menagerie*, *Habeas Corpus*, *Secret Thoughts*, *Oleanna* (Octagon, Bolton); *White Star of the North* (Lyric, Belfast); *Shoot the Crow* (Opera House, Belfast); *Snookered* (Bush, London); *The Killing of Sister George* (Arts, London); *Swampoodle* (Uline Arena, Washington DC); *Treemonisha* (Pegasus Opera UK tour); *A Slight Ache*, *Landscape* (National Theatre).

Recent lighting designs: *Vernon God Little* (Decadent Theatre, Galway Town Hall); *The Pillowman* (Gaiety, Dublin); *Pentecost*, *The Little Prince* (Lyric, Belfast); *Perseverance Drive* (Bush); *A Taste of Honey* (Hull Truck/national tour); *Philadelphia, Here I Come!* (Lyric, Belfast); *Wanted! Robin Hood*, *Arabian Nights* (Lowry, Salford); *Much Ado about Nothing* (Royal Shakespeare Company, Stratford-upon-Avon/West End).

Ciaran won the 2014 Best Lighting Design at the Irish Times Theatre Awards for *Pentecost*.

Carl Kennedy – Sound Design

Carl trained at Academy of Sound in Dublin. Previous work with Prime Cut includes *After Miss Julie, Scarborough, Black Milk, Secret City, Kaleidoscope, The Baths, Still Life Still* and *Right Here Right Now*. He has been a composer/sound designer on one hundred theatre productions, working with venues and companies including the Abbey, the Gaiety Theatre, the Lyric Theatre, ANU Productions, Rough Magic, Decadent, Fishamble, Theatre Lovett, Speckintime, Gúna Nua, Loose Canon, Peer to Peer, Siren, Broken Crow, Randolf SD, and Theatre Makers. He has been nominated three times for the Irish Times Theatre Award for Best Sound Design. He also composes music and sound design for video games; titles include *Leonardo and His Cat, Curious George, Curious about Shapes and Colors, Jelly Jumble, Too Many Teddies* and *Dino Dog*. TV credits include sound design for *16 letters* (Independent Pictures/RTÉ) and SFX editing and foley recording for *Centenary* (RTÉ).

Nicola Curry – Movement Director

Nicola is founder and Artistic Director of Maiden Voyage Dance. She has commissioned and produced over twenty-five new works from national and international choreographers and collaborators. Previous Prime Cut credits include *Scorch* (2015); *I Am My Own Wife* (2012); *Shoot the Crow* (2011); *Scarborough* (2010); along with community performance projects *Still Life Still* (2011); and *Right Here, Right Now* (2010). Nicola was the recipient of the 2014 Spirit of Festival Award from the Belfast Festival at Queen's.

Oona Doherty – Movement Consultant

Oona trained at St Louise's Comprehensive Belfast, London School of Contemporary Dance, University of Ulster and Laban London.

She has worked internationally since 2010 in collaboration with dance companies such as: TRASH Netherlands, Veronika Riz Italy, Abattoir Ferme Belgium, Emma martin/United Fall Dublin and most recently with Landmark Productions on Enda Walsh's *Arlington*.

Her choreography, *Hope Hunt and Hard to Be Soft* (*part one*) – A Belfast Prayer in Four Parts is touring Ireland 2016/17
www.oonaodhertyweb.com

Enda Kenny – Costume Design

Enda has been working in costume departments in film and theatre since graduating with a degree in model-making and design in 2003. He specialises in costume design, textile art, millinery and prop costume.

Previous film and TV productions include HBO's *Game of Thrones, Pirates of the Caribbean 2* and *The Golden Compass*. He has also produced work for various West End shows in London for the National Theatre, ENO and The Royal Opera House, Covent Garden.

PRIME CUT PRODUCTIONS

Established in 1992, Prime Cut Productions is an Independent Theatre Producing Organisation based in Belfast and is one of Northern Ireland and the island of Ireland's leading theatre companies. Prime Cut Productions are committed to producing excellent contemporary theatre that is accessible and entertaining for as wide an audience as possible, forge artistic links locally and internationally and continue to nurture the development of theatre practice and artists in Northern Ireland. Prime Cut have produced forty highly acclaimed Northern Irish premieres of the best of International Theatre as well showcasing the work of Northern Irish Theatre Artists across the island of Ireland and beyond.

In 2013 Prime Cut completed a four-year international collaboration with East West Theatre, Sarajevo and Mladinsko Theatre, Ljubljana that culminated in a European tour of an ambitious large-scale multi-disciplinary Theatre Production that featured a Community Engagement Programme of over 500 people from Northern Ireland, Bosnia and Slovenia. In 2014–15 our production of the *Chilean Trilogy* was named by The Stage UK as one of its Top 10 UK Productions, we were the recipients of the BBC Performing Arts Fellowship, the Weston Jerwood Creative Bursary, our Chair won the Allianz Arts & Business Board Member of the Year Award and our Artistic Director Emma Jordan was awarded the Breakthrough Award for Cultural Entrepreneurship by the Paul Hamlyn Foundation and the Spirit of Festival by Belfast International Arts Festival. In 2016 our production of Stacey Gregg's *Scorch* won both the Irish Times Irish Theatre Award for Best New Play and a Writer's Guild Award for Best New Script.

Artistic Director	Emma Jordan
Executive Producer	Una Nic Eoin
Outreach Manager	Matt Faris
Finance Officer	Lorriane McBrearty
Audience Development Manager	Conn McKermott
Artistic Associates	Ciaran Bagnall, Louise Lowe and Rhiann Jeffrey
Board of Directors	Chris Bailey [Chair], Peter Ballance, Chris Glover, Kathy Hayes, Edel Magill, Georgia Simpson, Michelle Young

Prime Cut Productions, 5th Floor, The MAC, 10 Exchange St West, Belfast, BT1 2NJ
T_ 028 9024 4004 E_ info@primecutproductions.co.uk
www. primecutproductions.co.uk

Prime Cut Chronology

1992: Irish premiere of Jim Cartwright's *Two*, directed by Simon Magill, Old Museum Arts Centre, Belfast and national tour.

1992: Northern Irish premiere of Athol Fugard's *A Place with the Pigs*, directed by Simon Magill, Old Museum Arts Centre, Belfast and national tour. Ger Ryan winner of EMA Best Actress Award.

1994: Irish premiere of Ariel Dorfman's *Death and the Maiden*, directed by Simon Magill, Old Museum Arts Centre, Belfast.

1995: Northern Irish premiere of David Mamet's *Oleanna*, directed by Simon Magill, Old Museum Arts Centre, Belfast and tour of Northern Ireland.

1996: World premiere of Trevor Griffiths' *Who Shall Be Happy?*, Old Museum Arts Centre, Belfast, and national and international tour. Stanley Townsend winner of TMA Best Actor Award.

1996: April Sunday's Festival of New Writing, a co-production with Tinderbox Theatre Company.

1997: Company change name from Mad Cow Productions to Prime Cut Productions.

1997: Irish premiere of Sam Shepard's *Simpatico*, directed by Jackie Doyle, Old Museum Arts Centre, Belfast and national tour. Niamh Linehan nominated for Irish Times Best Supporting Actress Award.

1997: European premiere of Daniel Danis' *Stone and Ashes*, directed by Jackie Doyle, Old Museum Arts Centre, Belfast and national tour.

1998/9: Irish premiere of Cindy Lou Johnston's *Brilliant Traces*, directed by Jackie Doyle, Old Museum Arts Centre, Belfast and the Lyric Theatre, Belfast, and national tour.

1998: Northern Irish premiere of Clare McIntyre's *Low Level Panic*, directed by Jackie Doyle, Old Museum Arts Centre, Belfast, and tour of Northern Ireland.

1998: Women's writing workshop with Clare McIntyre.

1999: Irish premiere of George Walker's *Criminal Genius*, Old Museum Arts Centre, Belfast

1999: April Sunday's co-production with Tinderbox Theatre Company and Centre des Auteurs Dramatique, Montreal.

2000: Irish premiere of George Walker's *Problem Child*, Old Museum Arts Centre, Belfast, and national tour, Maria Connolly nominated for Irish Times Best Actress Award.

2000: Irish premiere of Patrick Marber's *Dealer's Choice* directed by Tim Loane, the Lyric Theatre, Belfast, and tour of Northern Ireland. Dan Gordon nominated for TMA Best Supporting Actor Award.

2000: Writers' Residency Programme, Tyrone Gutherie Centre, Annamakherig.

2001: European premiere of Michel Marc Bouchard's *Coronation Voyage*, directed by Jackie Doyle, Waterfront Hall, Belfast.

2001: Irish premiere of Edward Albee's *Three Tall Women*, directed by Jackie Doyle, Lyric Theatre, Belfast, and national tour. Kate O'Toole winner of TMA Best Actress Award.

2001: Northern Irish premiere of Mark Ravenhill's *Shopping and F***ing*, directed by Jackie Doyle, Old Museum Arts Centre, Belfast, and national tour.

2002: Northern Irish premiere of David Mamet's *American Buffalo*, directed by Jackie Doyle, Lyric Theatre, Belfast, and national tour.

2002: William Shakespeare's *Macbeth*, directed by Jackie Doyle, a co-production with the Lyric Theatre, Belfast, and national tour.

2002: World premiere of *The Chance*, Peter Carey's story adapted for the stage by Jackie Doyle produced in association with the Belfast Festival at Queen's.

2003: Irish premiere of Timberlake Wertenbaker's *After Darwin*, directed by Jackie Doyle, The Project, Dublin and the Old Museum Arts Centre, Belfast.

2003: Irish premiere of Gregory Burke's *Gagarin Way*, directed by Jackie Doyle, Old Museum Arts Centre, Belfast, and national tour.

2004: *Ashes to Ashes* by Harold Pinter and *The Mercy Seat* by Neil LaBute, Lyric Theatre, Belfast.

2005: World premiere of *Cold Comfort*, written and directed by Owen McCafferty Old Museum Arts Centre, Belfast, in association with Theatre503, London.

2006: Samuel Beckett's *Endgame*, in association with the Waterfront Hall Studio, Belfast, directed by Mark Lambert. Staged reading of Beckett's *All That Fall*, Waterfront Hall Studio. Monica Frawley nominated for Best Designer Irish Times Awards.

2006: Irish premiere of Naomi Wallace's *The Trestle at Pope Lick Creek*, directed by Patrick O' Kane, Old Museum Arts Centre, Belfast, and national tour.

2007: Irish premiere of Owen McCafferty's *Scenes from the Big Picture*, directed by Conall Morrison – Waterfront Hall Studio, Belfast, nominated for Best Production and Best Lighting Design [Nick McCall] Irish Times Awards.

2008: Irish premiere of Dennis Kelly's *After the End*, directed by Emma Jordan, Old Museum Arts Centre, Belfast.

2008: World premiere of Sophocles' *Antigone* in a new version written and directed by Owen McCafferty, Ulster Bank Belfast Festival at Queen's. Walter McMonagle nominated for Best Supporting Actor Irish Times Awards.

2009: Northern Irish premiere of Marina Carr's *Woman and Scarecrow*, directed by Emma Jordan, Old Museum Arts Centre, Belfast, and national tour. Gina Moxley nominated for Best Actress Irish Times Awards.

2009: Irish Premiere of Vassily Sigarev's *Black Milk* directed by Matt Torney for the Ulster Bank Festival at Queen's.

2009: Community Engagement production with Ardoyne Women's Group and New Lodge Arts – *The Heights* by Lisa Magee directed by Alison McCrudden. Old Museum Arts Centre, Belfast.

2010: Irish Premiere of *Scarborough* by Fiona Evans directed by Emma Jordan, site-responsive production, produced in association with the MAC.

2010: Community Engagement production written and directed by Louise Lowe and Matt Faris Baby Grand Opera House, Belfast.

2010: Irish premiere of *Vincent River* by Phillip Ridley directed by Sophie Motley: Crescent Arts Centre and island wide tour

2011: Northern Irish premiere of *Shoot the Crow* by Owen McCafferty directed by Emma Jordan.

2011 Community Engagement production written and directed by Louise Lowe and Matt Faris, The Assembly Rooms, Belfast.

2011: Northern Irish premiere of *Blackbird* by David Harrower, directed by Emma Jordan: Lyric Naughton Studio and NI tour.

2012: Revival of *Shoot The Crow* by Owen McCafferty, directed by Emma Jordan: Grand Opera House Belfast and Ireland-wide tour.

2012: Community Engagement production *The Baths* directed by Louise Lowe – Templemore Baths, Belfast.

2012: Northern Irish premiere of Doug Wright's *I Am My Own Wife* in a co-production with The MAC, directed by Emma Jordan – The MAC, Belfast.

2013: Community Engagement production *Kaleidoscope* directed by Louise Lowe – Belfast City Centre.

2013: *The Conquest of Happiness* co-created by Emma Jordan & Haris Pasovic in a co-production with East West Theater, Sarajevo and Mladinsko Theatre, Ljubljana – commissioned for 2013 Derry – City of Culture UK and European tour.

2014: *The Chilean Trilogy – Villa & Discurso* by Guilermo Calderon directed by Roisin McBrinn and *Tejas Verdes* directed by Sophie Motley in a co-production with The MAC Belfast. (Included in The Stage UK's Top 10 Productions 2014.)

2014: The REVEAL Programme launched to support and develop the work of emerging NI Theatre Artists.

2015: *God of Carnage* by Yasmina Reza directed by Emma Jordan in a co-production with The MAC, Belfast.

2015: *Mydidae* by Jack Thorne directed by Rhiann Jeffrey (REVEAL Artist and BBC Performing Arts Fellow) in association with The MAC. Ulster Bank International Arts Festival.

2015: *Scorch* by Stacey Gregg directed by Emma Jordan in association with The MAC and Outburst Queer Arts Festival.

2016: *After Miss Julie* by Patrick Marber directed by Emma Jordan in association with The MAC.

2016: *Scorch* by Stacey Gregg, UK & Ireland tour directed by Emma Jordan.

SCORCH

Stacey Gregg

'Gender fraud' and Discussion
Stacey Gregg

When I began writing *Scorch*, the first cases of 'gender fraud' appeared to involve cisgender female teens. But as more cases occurred, some involving trans men, I needed to ensure the story was being told carefully. There are limitations to that as I am not transgender, and the idea of cisplaining makes my blood run cold. So we consulted transmasculine groups and non-binary advisers and had a talkback with people from across the gender spectrum.

When it came to publishing the play, I was initially reluctant as I didn't want to put another traumatic story out there, and I really want this story to date fast. But it might not. And there might be young people out there who don't go to theatres but who might get their hands on this. So we've gathered some activists and more voices here to discuss these cases and what it means to them.

Trans Media Watch

We've followed a number of case of so-called 'gender fraud' over the past few years and have spoken with court staff, journalists and some of those directly affected about this issue. We have seen people's lives turned upside down in situations very much like the one Kes experiences in the play – people who were simply being themselves and did not imagine that they could be doing anything wrong. It's particularly difficult for trans people to declare their trans status when they don't know that that's how society understands them. It's worrying that being trans is treated like this when, as the play notes, other things are not – not only does it imply that there's something bad about being trans, it implies that it's the worst possible secret a person could keep. We don't believe that most reasonable people would agree with that.

Although we have had some success in persuading individual journalists and programme-makers to handle this issue more sensitively, most of the press is still fixated on the idea that it's all about predatory lesbians and deception. This illustrates the level of homophobia still present in media culture, and it's very difficult to tackle. It encourages transphobia and potentially also creates dangers for intersex people, whose bodies may differ from what partners expect.

We are always available to help journalists who find themselves struggling with issues like this. It's really important to get it right because the media shapes public discourse and that, ultimately, shapes the way that people are treated by the law.

This play is doing its bit to move society in a more humane direction, and we're grateful for it.

Professor Alex Sharpe, School of Law, Keele University, LLB, LLM, PhD, Barrister

In recent years, trans and gender-queer kids have been convicted of sexual offences on the basis of 'gender fraud'. Most have received a custodial sentence, in one case eight years, and all have been placed on the Sex Offenders Register. These cases are a cause for concern, not only because desire-led intimacy ought not to be regulated through the criminal law, but because trans and gender-queer kids are singled out for special attention. Sexual encounters are always preceded by imperfect information about lovers, yet law, in the main, considers apparent consent valid. However, the problems with these kinds of prosecutions run deeper than legal doctrine. 'Gender fraud' narratives are ultimately about cis power and privilege. Their central motif, 'deception', functions both to wound ontologically and to foster misunderstanding of trans and gender-queer lives, as well as the motivations of young people exploring their gender and sexuality.

Scorch forces us to see things from the point of view of Kes, a young person whose emerging gender identity, embodied and real though it is, does not lend itself easily to our impoverished 'either/or' mindset. The play leaves us with discomforting though important questions.

Ruth McCarthy, Outburst Queer Arts Festival Director

The question I get asked most often in relation to Outburst is 'Why do you use the word "Queer"?' I'm never sure how to answer without getting overly enthusiastic about certain artists or activists and insisting that someone leaves with a stack of 45s from Outpunk Records piled up to their chin. But to talk about *Scorch* is to talk about Queer, so I'll try.

Queer is an unapologetic celebration of difference, a non-judgemental recognition of human beings in all our complexities and contradictions. It is not always clear-cut or binary; it is challenging and suggests that questions are often far more useful, and far more interesting, than answers.

When I first read *Scorch*, what struck me most was not just the raw beauty of the language but also the realisation of Queer. *Scorch* doesn't offer tidy answers. It has instead a compassionate understanding of the spaces we need to allow each other to sit with questions.

Outburst is fiercely committed to supporting the development of new queer theatre and to partnering with writers and companies who can bring queer work to life for a whole new generation. In Stacey and Prime Cut, Outburst has found natural and generous allies who offer us fresh understanding of what Queer is at a time and in a place where perhaps we need it most.

Naomhán O'Connor, non-binary transgender activist

When I was approached by Outburst Arts to consult on *Scorch*, I was initially quite wary. Stories about transgender people are so often misrepresentative of our community that I was cautious of getting involved. However, I was sent the script to read in advance of meeting the actors and director and my fears were assuaged. This story of a gender-questioning teenager resonated so strongly with me that it could have been my story that was being told.

The bodies and gender expression of trans people, both young and old, are continually being policed by society. Our stories are most often told through the cisgender gaze so as to highlight our difference from 'the norm'. As a writer and an activist, Stacey has been very careful in her research to ensure that the story does not sensationalise or delegitimise the trauma that so many young trans people experience.

If you are a transgender or non-binary or gender-questioning person reading this play, angered that yet another cisgender writer is telling our story, I say this to you: Give it a chance. This story might just touch a nerve in a way that you didn't think possible for a cisgender person to reach.

If you are a cisgender person, remember that our stories are best told by those who have the lived experience of being scorned by society for living our truth. Stacey, through her desire to tell the truth of our experience rather than telling the most sensationalised story, has managed to create a masterpiece that cuts to the bone. Remember that real people have been treated this way, and consider your attitudes towards our community before policing us.

That trans people are being forced to out themselves before becoming intimate with another person is a violation of our basic right to privacy. The issue is not with our bodies, the issue is with society's perpetuation of a norm that simply does not exist. We have become so obsessed with genitals that we have forgotten that we are all basically the same: humans with emotions.

Fox Fisher, artist, film-maker and campaigner

The reporting of the incidents involving Gemma Barker, Gayle Newland, Chris Wilson, Kyran Lee or Justine McNally are complicated on many levels. For most people, it may seem clear cut, especially if they followed each case through the mainstream media.

However, rarely has the accused been given an interview. In the case of Gemma Barker, a documentary gave platform to the two girls who had been deceived, and their family, about what had happened. I cannot really say what actually went through Gemma's mind or why they did what they did. That's something only they can say. I am intrigued to hear everyone's perspective and the intention behind what they did.

In this digital age we live in with all the social platforms and social media, technology has enabled many people, particularly trans people, to exist as an avatar which may be more fitting that the body we currently inhabit. Is this deceit? For some trans people, living as their true selves online is the only option that we have. We are not able to express ourselves or come out and live our true and authentic lives, so look to online platforms in order to explore and find a way to exist as who we truly are. And I don't think this is something only trans people do, I think it's something a lot of people do for a variety of reasons.

Maybe Justine or Gayle or Gemma didn't have the words or the agency to formulate or explain their own identity and this was the only way for them to try and desperately express who they are and what they felt like. For someone who is ashamed of who they are, perhaps acceptance and support may have created less risk-taking and extreme behaviour. Trans people don't want to be judged or made to feel less than human. When you're raised in a society that has such rigid gender roles and enforces heteronormativity, it can be so hard and traumatising to try and navigate your way through it when you don't fit in. It's like everyone else got a manual on how to behave, what to do and how to feel and you're the only one who didn't receive it in the post.

So in each case, we are looking at many different aspects that haven't necessarily been explored. What do these cases tell us about gender and identity? Does this punishment have underlying homophobic implications, since they were all discovered to be assigned female at birth? Without justifying what they did, it's an important aspect that needs to be weighed in. Because we all do things for a reason. If the reason Chris, Kyran, Justine et al. did all this is because they didn't have the agency, opportunity or knowledge to formulate and explain their own identity, it's a problem that we as a society need to fix. We also need to look into where we stand with education about sexuality, sexual health, consent, body image and more.

We need to realise that there are so many things we aren't talking about and that we are not doing well enough. There are so many conversations we are not having with young people today that could make people understand boundaries, consent, different identities and experiences.

What's behind this is a culture that views trans people as something no one would ever want to be and it creates a never ending pit of self-hate for trans people who feel they don't match with the sex and gender they were assigned at birth. Some of us are so ashamed and have such deeply embedded hate for ourselves that we'd rather do anything we can to hide that fact and therefore try to either deny it or take it to extremes by trying to pass as a cis person. To them, being trans is something so awful, that they'd never want to live in a world that would view them in that way; as freaks.

Again, I'm not excusing any sort of aggressive behaviour or sexual abuse. However, to be completely marginalised and outcast from society for who you are, makes you do messed-up things and really affects your mental well-being on many levels. And something's not right when a judge gives more lenient sentences to paedophiles than he did to Gayle Newland.

If trans people were accepted in society, they wouldn't feel the need to look to online forums or create online identities because they could truly live out their true and authentic lives in society. But right now, this isn't a reality for most trans people. Things are thankfully moving forward and I truly believe we can reach that point, but right now we aren't treating trans people right and we aren't making sure everyone feels accepted and has the opportunity to be who they are.

These types of stories could be about any queer person that is ashamed of their sexuality or gender identity, which then spiralled into something out of hand as a way to mask their own identity. This could have been me. This could've been my partner Owl (who is also trans). This could've been anyone. This is what can happen when we live in a society that makes people feel ashamed of who they are. This is what can happen when we don't have those conversations.

Support and Further Resources

www.stonewall.org.uk/help-advice
Switchboard LGBT+ helpline, *tel:* 0300 330 0630
genderedintelligence.co.uk
Samaritans *tel:* 116 123 (UK & ROI) *email*: jo@samaritans.org

Great care has been taken to avoid undermining the women who believed they were in relationships with men in these cases, but there are still lots of questions. We have a way to go to be able to talk about these cases in nuanced public discourse. We need to be able to hold lots of dissenting voices at once to ensure we're looking after everyone equally.

S.G.

Note on Performance

Scorch was inspired by recent UK cases.

This is an invitation to distance the audience gently from a literal performance of a character by incorporating metaphor into the production. If clothing is used, try to avoid a literal association with the concept of drag. Minimal set and props are advised. Throughout, consider casting members of the audience as players in Kes's journey. Engage and make eye contact with them. Stage directions are for guidance but open to interpretation.

The performance leaves room for interpretation. Some see *Scorch* as dealing with LGBTQIA concerns, some with trans, some with a general duty of care towards young people, and this may be reflected in casting. The dissensus is deliberate.

Scorch was developed with support from Anchor and Buoys NI. In the original production the voices of local young people from these groups were incorporated on pages 34–5.

Huge thanks to Stef O'Driscoll, Amy Conroy, Naomhán O'Connor, all those at Anchor and Buoy, Suzanne Bell, Ellie Kendrick and Amy McAllister.

S.G.

'There is no original or primary gender a drag imitates, but gender is a kind of imitation for which there is no original.'

Judith Butler

'Get away from her you bitch'
https://youtu.be/RDqTwSO1DDc

Character

KES

This text went to press before the end of rehearsals and so may differ slightly from the play as performed.

(*A young person, warm, nervous energy. This is* KES. *Maybe we don't identify them as the audience congregate.*)

(*Perhaps the audience form a circle, of which* KES *is part.*)

(*For some time we are* KES*'s mirror as* KES *unselfconsciously examines the reflected body.*)

(*As* KES *imitates the body language of audience-members-as-reflection.*)

(*As* KES *dances to music*)

(*maybe*)

(*camply*)

(*maybe*)

(*as we have all done alone.*)

(*Then:*)

The suede waistcoat is my favourite.

Brown suede.

Um.

I have a waistcoat with elephants stitched on it too.

And I have a silky waistcoat.

With cats on it.

Maybe mice.

Not sure.

I am a 'deb-bon-air eight-year-old' Granda says.

I have a bouncy-ball collection.

I'm shaping up to be a real ah, 'heartbreaker' Granda says.

He called the self-service machine in *Tescos* 'young lady' though, so…

(*Brightly*.) I have lots of waistcoats. I love them.

(*Thinks*.)

Try weeing standing up.

Yeah. Wee standing up.

I have a brother and boy cousins, so um, think it's cos I haven't tried.

I'm wearing cords. Stand at the toilet. Confident. Then this stain, down my favourite blue corduroys. Hide them in the rockery.

Wonder what Mum thinks when she digs them up.

'That is not a carrot,' probably.

Uhm.

Wake up and boobs. You know? Like, no one asked me. Just pop up overnight. Like in *Alien*. The film? With Sigourney Weaver? Only out of my chest. Twice: (*Demonstrates*.) pft. Pft.

Want to give them back thank you bye.

I'm a boy. Then eleven. Then boobs.

High school's okay. It's okay. In high school I have the same friends. Climb trees, football, et cetera et cetera tomboy grow-out-of-it phase et cetera.

Try being girly.

Try to – Thirteen. Lipgloss. Quite excited. Free with a magazine about. Ponies or something. Try to – try to drop 'boyfy' into conversation.

'Boyfy.'

Do people say 'boyfy'? Or is it like when I tried to say 'oke' but it turns out it's 'O'–'K' as in the same as O –K–A–Y and you don't say it 'oke' it's not like a cool way of saying it, it just looks that way before anyone tells you it's not.

'Boyfy.'

(*Maybe* KES *tries the lipgloss, then tries saying 'boyfy'*.)

'Boyfy.'

Boyfy.

Boyfy.

Boyfy.

Boyfy.

Boyfy.

Boyfuh.

Boyfah.

Boyf.

Buh

(*Until there is an absurd amount of lipgloss*.)

(*Until 'boyfy' sounds absurd*.)

Try it. But. Feel daft. Pretending. I'm pretending. Get bored.

...

Bioshock. Minecraft. Black Ops. The Last of Us Assassins
Creed HaloGrandTheftAuto WatchDogs

Gaming online. I am twelve, thirteen, fourteen.

Always choose the coolest avatar, always dudes. If not,
a mushroom. But usually dudes. Gaming stuff, made by dudes.
All the characters are dudes. Never even think about it. Just,
normal. You can be whatever you want.

(*Sings enthusiastically*.) Whatever whatever whatever you
waaaaant.

BLEEP.

Her name equals bleep.

Never answer straight away, no one likes a keeno. Think
you're just waiting like some kind of nut, which we both are
obviously. Bleep: 'Hi yah.' Jules calls it Player Ready Twitch

haha. Jules is funny. She has a cool tattoo a line from *Jurassic Park* but it's cool. She loves Leonard Cohen. And eyeliner. And gifs. We're always laughing at stupid things. Little cry-y emoticon faces hahaha.

Okay.
Okay.
Okay.

(*Full house lights. We are a support group.*)

I'm trying to say it from the top.
Everything. Okay?
Okay.
Cool cool coooool. Just, channel someone cool. David Bowie or, Fiona Bruce.

She is pretty bloody cool.

Make eye contact with the circle.

We sit in a circle.

A circle is about trust.

A square, well a square is for fascists, obviously. A circle is for trust.

Laugh HAHAHA not like a maniac, but enough so you all know I know it's funny, me and my waistcoats. Some people take themselves too seriously. Life's too awesome not to laugh, you know?

Look round the circle and you're nodding.

You *get* it.

Feel another surge of. Of of – wonder if it's cool to talk about how *happy* I am. Cos some of you guys are having a crappy time. You have to come here to talk about the crappy time you're having. Wonder if I do belong here, cos I actually just want to share how happy I am.

I have a girl. Yeah.

And this circle needs a sprinkle of joy. And I want to be that sprinkler, said the bishop to the the thing.

My girl. Jules.

Er, I do wonder if liking girls means I am... un homo. But I don't know any real ones yet... just convince myself I'll probably get a boyfriend one day, like, when I have to. I am quite convincing.

Oh, there's this movie – watch it a zillion times – this guy dresses as a girl to get the girl. I *love* that movie. Flippin hilarious. Hi-lar-i-ous. This guy looks amazing. Scientific fact: men look AMAZING in make-up.

I don't get why, but I'm a bit obsessed with that movie.

I think... I think I watch movies different.

Like. I watch movies through the dude's point of view.

Thought everyone did.

Like, everyone thinks I *fancy* Ryan Gosling. I want to *be* him. Duh. I want to be Ryan. And sometimes the girl. And sometimes Ryan. And sometimes – (*Overwhelmed.*) Wah stroke! Ryan is completely hot. He'd rock an elephant waistcoat.

Me and Jules've been messaging for years. Up till crazy o'clock messaging. About Laser Eyes. Laser Eyes her fascist mum. About like, how Jules hopes she'll be the first one to go to college and. And she thinks I'm a guy.

And I don't correct her. Don't correct her cos I *am* Kes.

Kes, like the kid on the front of that Ken Loach film. I love that picture. Haven't seen the film, it's old but. The kid smiling and the bird? Love it. Love my name. Kes. Everything's – Think about a name like... 'Jonny'. But that's just, crap.

(*Maybe text appears.*)

'U R SUCH A SWEET GUY'

(KES *thinks. Not for too long. Then –*)

Smiley face.

'WISH I COULD HANG OUT WIV U'

Emoticon emoticon emoticon no exclamation marks.

Exclamation marks are needy.

'HOT'

New Profile. MALE. FIFA. Snowboarding. JJ Abrams. People Like what I Like. Feeds totally different – different ads, different colours. Cool. I Like that they Like that I Like what they Like! Jake in school created an account where he was a Chair our teachers sit in and all his updates were like: 'agh stop your bum is squashing me!!!' Funniest thing EVER we all nearly died.

Jake the Chair Ha.

Jake was a Chair.

Bleep.

Jules wants to Skype.

Oh

my

word.

Oh my wordy word.

We only ever texted.

Bellytwist, flying over hills superfast in the car something dilating heart a balloon inflating head hanging out window blasting go faster 'yes okay ten o'clock okay?'

K, cool.

Welded to seat. Anticipation-locked Z-shaped at laptop barricade bedroom no I DON'T want lasagne Mum I'm BUSY.

You know –

You know –

all those funny movies where the guy goes to crazy lengths to prove how much he loves the girl, like pretend to be a priest or professional dancer or hypnotise her and eventually, even when he comes clean, the girl is just so moved and happy he loves her she's just like: 'alright!' and they just kiss and the credits go up?

(*Maybe canned laughter.*)

Pinching things from Dad. From my brother.

Shirt.

Bart Simpson boxers – so much funner than girls' stuff – stash them in my laundry box

heart like *dut-dut dut-dut DUT-DUT DUT-DUT*

model myself on cool guys. Not like, some crap guy in a fleece.

(*Maybe* KES *strikes a few poses.*)

Been collecting Topman models. Gangstas. Dandys. Normalcore. Metro-boys. Everyone thinks it's a crush-book, but it's actually my reference document.

I'm testing out holding a *wallet*, like *lads* do.

In my more modest dreams Bill Murray and Justin Bieber bop me on the shoulder in a dude way and I say something showbizzy like: 'HEY, WATCH IT, BRO!'

Take photos. Look at myself.

Do I look flat in this?

My body. Outline. I look.

Cool.

Perfect.

Player One Ready.

Practise how I stand. (*Does so.*)

Sit. (*Does so.*)

Voice. Read on a forum you shouldn't overdo it. Sound like Aslan or something.

(KES *is emerging before our eyes*.)

Hang out on forums as Kes. Like. Tumblr. Cute Boys Who Are Girls. Photostream. Like like like search like like bookmark like like.

People like me. There're people like me on there.

Tonnes. In Portland. Milton Keynes. Belfast.*

Heart burning like darkest Mordor – surely these are weirdos? I'm not like them, right? Right? I'm not weird. They're the lost, the curious, the, the *Great British Bake Off* fans, everyone needs somewhere to go, somewhere to think in capitals

Me too.

Step through. Portals to the World the World for Kes nothing impossible NOTHING you can't stick a cat on and turn into a snazzy gif – no longer lumpish I'm a careless queen, a cad, lead in a crazy romcom, fingers shredding up the keyboard she's LOLing till her sides split I'm WINning –

Don't tell anyone, obviously.

Like the movie I watched over and over. Just know, I can't. Yet.

We only ever texted till now.

We Skype.

(*Maybe we hear the call tone*.)

(*It goes on for some time before* KES *has the courage to answer.*)

(*A rush. Some moments here*.)

(*Maybe we see the first step towards* KES.)

'Hi.'

Wait for her to – …

but. She doesn't. We just. Hang out.

---

* Change to whatever town or city the performance is taking place in.
  There is room here for judicious ad libbing.

Happiness. Aching, constant, consuming – on here it's. More real than real life. I'm honest on here. I'm being honest. This is important. This is it.

We Skype again.

Lie next to her face on my iPad in bed. Just. Laughing. Hanging. Just. Never felt so…

Friend.
Like.
Follow.

Jake was a bloody Chair it doesn't mean –

Wow.

Jules wants to *meet up*.

(*Swallows hard.*)

(*Deep breath.*)

Two train rides. Think I might spontaneously human combust.

I'm doing this I'm doing this don't think just just just

just

Her arm's in a sling. Barely speak. Terrified. She's so sweet. Think I'm gonna throw up it's amazing. We quote *Terminator 2*. I know all Edward Furlong's lines because I AM him.

(*Edward Furlong's actual voice.*) 'Mom, we need to be a little more constructive here, okay?'

Bop her in the face with my genius.

Hold hands.

Skin so soft.

I love her hand.

This is happening.

Her actual real hand in mine. Looks right in my actual real eyes. I look in hers.

We are like Paul McKenna.

In a mirror.

Can see me in her eyes. Tiny Keses in her lovely magic eyes.

She sees Kes.

She sees *me*.

…

Next time, strap down them pesky boobs. Bit sore, switch to a sports bra. Urg. Just want to squash them away. But, there they *are*. Just – wear baggy clothes. Scared she won't like me if I look too. Yuck. Feminine. Packing is when you put something down there, to feel, to feel like, comfy. You can get anything on the internet. (*Thinks*.) Baby lemurs in a bumbag, I don't know. Work in Asda, forty quid for a chest-binder is okay.

Don't go to great lengths.

But I'm passing.

She says I'm cute. *I'm cute*. ARGH. Eat two Toffee Crisps in celebration. Cannot believe it. I'm like those cartoons where their brain is literally made up of mini birds and hearts and biscuits and things. I mean kissing is like WOW. Just lying around in each other's arms: WOW. We just fit. Her – everything – just – WOW.

I mean, there are so many moments I think SHIT she is going to SAY something. Or, think, I need to say something. Especially at the start.

But.

Moments come and go.

Months come and go.

Her sixteenth.

We talk in… code. We argue in code. Want to talk about it but. Scared.

Guess, she knows, or. Prefers not asking. An understanding.
You know?

Stay over sometimes.

Talk about running away to New York together, where the
hipsters are. Make so many plans. Cos she knows, like I do,
something's gonna have to give. But, not yet.

Never asks why I only go in the disabled loo. (There's so many
men in men's loos.)

Why I never take my hat off.

But I reckon, we're both in Narnia together. That's half the thing.

Laser Eyes, her mother, does not like me. Laser Eyes is a blast
of ice, always flick flick flicking through her Avon brochures.

We. We uh. Sleep together. Amazing.

I – She

We are. We –

Worry a bit. Hurt her a bit, I think. She says go easy, and I do.
Neither of us totally know what we're doing, but she you know,
comes. I don't, cos it's for her. Want to be the perfect boyfriend.
Tell her how gorgeous she is. Make her come. Make sure
everything is ready. Pick the one that has the best reviews. Says
it's soft. Soft and realistic to touch, like a real ahm, cock, the
website says. Or, more specifically, Joan from Kent: (*Uptight*.)
'very pleasant.'

Don't know if we'd have gone this far only… we… we both are.

In love. She says she loves me. So. It's…

you don't use the. Thing. They're not actually for that. The ones
for packing, not… they're not strap-ons, not to use. Reckon you
graduate to that.

Read somewhere it doesn't matter how you um, do it – as long
as you are respectful, right?

Cringe, talk about getting married and stuff. Oh my goodness.
Nuts.

Soulmates.

Circle's nodding, listening. First time I'm saying any of this. Out
loud. To you. Now. Voluntarily. My voice, my. Makes it real. Feel
drunk, even though I don't really drink. Tell the, the – what? The
group. Whhoooosh. Feels AMAZING – to talk about it. Want to
feel this free every day. Like being online but in a real room with
mediocre instant coffee! Want to kiss kiss SNOG everyone in the
circle, not in a sexy way, just. Drunk on freedom. I'm Kes. Birds
spring from my heart feel I feel alive. Feel real. Thick with
weight and confidence radiates from my centre I have shoulders
I could cave a door in to help an old lady I'd be charming and
helpful and I wanna walk with my pack between my legs my
eyes squinting in the sun just like James flipping Franco and no
one will ask 'what are you?' I'm just a dude.

(*Quickly.*) Maybe not trans. Don't know.

Haven't worked it out yet.

Don't know.

But a cute boi. B-O-I. Boi. That's queer slang for cute girls that
look like boys.

I'm trying to improve my queer slang. I mean it's important
actually, cos male-to-female trans people are the butt of a lot of
lazy jokes. But transdudes are like, anti-comedy. This is crucial
info. Transvestites: funny. Men who want to be women: funny.
Women who are dudes:

not funny, apparently.

In the movies they get depressed or stalky or kill themselves in
burning houses.

Wonder why it is. People are weird.

In the circle there's a shy girl with a bad wig.

(*Aside to whoever is next to them.*) This bad, blonde wig. She'll
never pass. She'll never pass with that flippin wig. Mate. Want

to tell him – tone it down. Looks shit. But – that'd be a mean.
Don't want to be mean. So I don't. Say she looks sweet. And,
she does, really. She's all like: 'Emmylou is da bomb, chicken.'

(Emmylou's the wig)

Jules messages, says I lied to her,

which,

I don't think I did,

lie,

but she won't answer my calls.

Not picking up.

Sends the odd message, but.

(*Puzzled, hurt silence*.)

It's cool.

Hurts. Miss her. Miss us.

But.

Don't know – kind of like being heartbroken. Once I stop
crying. Least I get someone to be heartbroken about. Not
everyone gets that. Still feel lucky. And just think: I'm not on
the outside any more. I'm *in* life. I'm Ryan Gosling in *Drive* but
minus the homicidal stampy scene that literally made me choke
on a Malteser.

Trying to get over Jules. It sucks but I feel. Feel –

(*Maybe now, an impossibly accomplished movement sequence: this is how it feels to be fully bodily present and realised*.)

Come to the meet-up group a second time. Read about T. Testosterone. But don't know. I'm just curious. Maybe cos I feel more, more – confident. Know how perfect it can feel.

If I transition maybe I can rock up on Jules' doorstep and offer her everything I can't offer her now. I can be her boyfriend. And we could be together. AND GET A CAT.

But but but it's another level and, it kinda I dunno it kinda s-s-scares me.

(*Back in the group*.)

The group properly sits up. This is what they love. Who gives a toot about lezzers? Boooooring. This is way better. And I'm ready to talk now. I've come to this group. Crapping myself but I found this group, LGBTQABCDEFG and this is a group where we start by letting the group know if we are she, he, they

BLOWS MY MIND.

'They. Prefer not to define.'

(KES*'s head implodes*.) Click.

Universe falls into place. He, she, they. And loads of words I don't even understand –

I can never concentrate in school but I'm learning *loads* here –

And we nod and use the right pronoun and I, I exist in the circle. Breathe, sit up in your seat, crack jokes, look people in the eyeballs.

And you shouldn't say tranny actually. Cos it's hurtful.

You can buy T online.

(KES *is coherent and technicolour, electric with discovery*.)

Max, this skinny dude in the circle next to a boy in completely gay loafers has been on hormones for months and you can totally see. He. Looks. Awesome. I'd never want to be one of those stacked dudes, but Max just looks *solid*. Great shoulders, and I don't know if he binds or what, but he looks like he's already had top surgery.

Can't stop looking at his body. His jaw.

T makes your boobs shrink. Your face more angular. Your voice drops. You lose fat off your hips and get more muscley. First thing I'd do is buzz off my hair. Short back and sides. Slick into a smart side parting. Sharp. Phwoar!

But shut up, shut up brain, getting carried away. Don't really know if I would. Just tucked my hair into a hat with Jules. Miss Jules. Would I miss my hair?

Like it long sometimes.

Don't tell anyone. Don't tell anyone that before I go home, I stop in a public toilet. Stuff my hat in my bag. Change. Don't feel trapped, just...

not there yet. Or something. Growing into it. Carry it around like it'll explode over some unsuspecting teacher when I'm in Normal Life Mode – buying shoes / eating McCoys / at Asda. Hide – go home someone else. Fraud. Some strange chick who wears a bridesmaid dress to her cousin's wedding.

I'm trying to find the opposite of lying. Um. The truth, I suppose. I know I don't say it right but don't know how... don't know how I can do it right yet.

The circle listen to Lara, a really pretty, hilarious transwoman. Lara's talking about disclosure and stealth and stuff. I feel lucky. Lara's saying she finally loves herself, and now she's ready to be loved. Now she's ready to allow herself to be loved. Damn right. Cos she's gorgeous and everything.

I have an ex.

I've loved.

I'm normal.

(*A mobile ringtone.* KES, *curious*.)

Seven missed calls from Mum.

(*A gear change*.)

Get home. Drop my bag in the hall. They're sitting at the kitchen table. Go 'Hola, chicas.'

Mum's crying. What? Dad won't look at me.

What is it?

Stomach cold.

Where've you been?

Just out.

Piece of paper on the table.

(*A miniature kitchen table appears, upon which is a ludicrous bomb*.)

There's a piece of paper between them. There's a piece of paper and it has my name on it.

Not Kes. The other name.

Don't really know what a court summons is.

Don't really know what legal aid is.

Still don't really understand, don't understand a lot of things. I'm not the brightest spark at school. I'm a stupid moron obviously. And now obviously I'm not going back to school till this is over. The one thing I know is I loved Jules. And I want it to be over.

Kind of think it'll be like the movies. In the movie it'd all be over and there'd be tears but they'll hug me and say

(*Recorded movie voice*.) 'we love you just the way you are'

'we want you to be happy.'

'It's the twenty-first century.' We love you.

And. I think they do. I think they do still love me.

But it isn't. It isn't. Okay.

It isn't like the movies.

A girl can't be charged with raping another girl. FYI.

Nope.

Legal-aid man clicks his pen, repeats himself. Not really actually looking at me.

Clicky pen. Click. Click-click. Don't say much. Can't. Can't. Don't know. How to

I know, once the jury hears my story, once they ask Jules what really happened, without listening to old Laser Eyes, I know they'll see I've been the perfect boyfriend, respectful. That I love Jules. And she loved me, I mean she posted all the time about it. She chased *me*. This is messy I own up to that. I get that. That's not cool. And I am sorry. I'm sorry Jules is upset. But the language. The words. Feel. Alien. Weird as the lipgloss when I was thirteen.

Glues my mouth shut.

'Sexual assault by penetration.'

Sexual assault by p–

And fraud. *Fraud*. That's what Al Capone does, or mafiosos. (*Mafioso voice*.) 'Fraud.'

Fraud. Fraaaauuuuuuuuddd fraud. Fraud.

Fraud. Fraud. Fraud. Fraud.

Fraud.

Fraud.

Fraud.

Fra –

(*Maybe* KES *invites us to say it too*.)

But. It's not a joke. They're saying I um. Deceived Jules, by pretending to be a man to have um, sex with her.

Tricked her into it.

Ab–

abused her. Abuse.

Keep saying to them, ask Jules. Maybe she is angry, but she'll tell you. I'm still Kes. I am Kes. I'm more Kes than not. I wasn't 'pretending'.

Even now, talking to you – I know how it must sound.

(KES *glitches and disintegrates. The music heard when* KES *was fullest plays again only backward, warped.*)

(KES*'s movements are now involuntary, compulsive.*)

(*Maybe* KES *ends up across the floor or upside down or in a bin.*)

Dad waves his fag in the air to shoo it all away. Hear him in the kitchen, on the phone: (*Dad.*) 'Run this by me again. So you could be a fucking – a rapist, or have a record for GBH, or a wife, or be sterile, or have fucking HIV even – but you don't have to "disclose" that?'

Blobs of body parts. Heart hanging outside my body, punchbag. I'm pretty gross, right? Solicitor staring at me: what are you? Sorry. Mouth's glued shut. She says – what are you?

'Are you a Homosexual or are you Gender Disordered?'

Um. My body is this weird black hole I drag round? I got Cs in English I'm not good at words.

'Dysphoria?' What? I *wasn't* but...

Aliens. I'm none of those things. I'm seventeen. I don't know. I don't know. I see Kes in the mirror. Kes is real. I'm. I'm. I'm.

Maybe I am an alien?

(*Maybe we hear a ghostly Ripley in* Aliens*: 'Get away from her, you bitch!'*)

Dad asks why.

Asked myself that over and over.

My brother just patted me on the shoulder today. Just shatter, into liquid sadness across the lino. But he just sits here, with me. They're alright, my family. Just. Scared. They don't know there are hipsters and b-o-i boi's out there.

It's okay, cos the people at the court will know.

Some of the group, I know you see what's happening in the press. Only came once or twice, but you try to contact me. Send me that box of Milk Tray by Royal Mail.

Weird, but really thoughtful. Thank you.

But Kes is dead for now. Kes is evidence, exhibit A and B and C in separate plastic bags.

Scrambled. Lose my, my… Eyeballs on me. Stuck to me. I know what they're – they're thinking – they're thinking about – (*Small.*) about my private. Most private. My invisible, soft parts, rebuilt into an alien.

(*Maybe, around now, we become aware of sensational tabloid headlines screaming into our consciousness.*)

Papers make a big deal of the 'paraphernalia' Laser Eyes found in my stupid backpack.

'Paraphernalia.'

A cock and a sports bra.

They make me sound like a terrorist.

Mum and Dad're broke, trying to pay for everything –

Laser Eyes says Jules will never trust again.

God.

I've written apologies, to Jules, to Mum, Dad – sorry. Sorry. I I don't know why I. Don't know but I'm *so* sorry and I'm guilty –

(*A gear change*.)

Solicitor blinks.

Dad nods.

Guilty.

(*Realisation*.) I'm guilty. I am guilty.

I did those things. I did them.

(*A sob seizes* KES.) P-plead guilty.

(*Small*.) It was fingers and tongues. It wasn't what people think HUMILIATION UGH the papers say she said I hurt her? Is she okay? Plead guilty, just get it over with. A cross-examination would kill me dead. They'd be like: do you have anything to say? And I'd be like: no, I'm actually dead.

(*Maybe* KES *takes off a shoe and puts it to an ear*.)

(*Hands the other to an audience – Lara*.)

Lara calls.

She's like, 'What, are we meant to fill out a questionnaire before any kind of intimacy now? Any time I go into a bar or on a date I have to out myself? Really? Otherwise we might end up in prison?'

I don't know Lara.

'Imagine I'm a racist, and you convince me you're not Indian, and then I learn that's not just a cool suntan, you *are* Indian, did you rape me?'

Wh– I don't know.

'*Gender fraud?* This is just homophobia, Kessy.'

I don't know.

'What about if I sleep with a woman (God forbid) and then I'm like "Hiyaa I'm an undercover cop?" They do that all the time! So *that's* fraud.'

I don't know, Lara. I just want it over. Lara? Thanks for calling.

Press call me a lesbian. A lot.

Am I?

Probably.

Calculating lesbian. Predatory lesbian. Ugly. Masquerading. Dangerous. Callous lesbian.

Probably.

At court, try to look normal. Coat from New Look. Only makes things worse. Like I am even more deceitful for not at least having the decency to look butch. Think – cos I look like a girl, the idea I slept with a girl like a boy scares them.

Get that now.

Judge says. I took away Jules' freedom to choose sex with a man.

(*Slowly, finding the sense of it.*) Took away her freedom. To choose sex with a man.

Groomed her.

I – I didn't realise, sir. I didn't realise that's what I was doing. And I'm sorry for hurting her and I'll take the punishment. Plead guilty. It'll just be over, right?

Three and a half years.

Three and a half years.

Prison.

My name on the sex offender's register.

There was kid killed a gay guy the other day and he got three and a half years for murder.

Am I as evil as him?

(*Blackout.*)

(*From somewhere, a voice.*)

(*It could be live. It could be recorded. It could roam the room.*)

You want to gouge your sex off.
You want to cut your head off.
You want to make love to someone who loves you want to
never touch another human in case you are dangerous in case
you hurt them want to get fucked by a guy just so you can say
you have and maybe it would make you more normal

Want to be normal and don't want to be normal

Didn't feel like an alien before. Felt like Sigourney or maybe
Bishop but the world has told you in no uncertain terms that
you are the thing that blasted out of the guy's stomach that you
are not what. You are not. You are not.

Nought. A gap. A hole. An error.

You eat up your peripheries you are no longer aware of them
smoothly one by one until you are an unidentifiable entity and
when you were blank you felt free.

But you are still here. Still here. Still you. Still the same.

You're not flesh you're a voice.

Online you were most human. You are neither. You are many.

Maybe you are an alien.

Maybe you are Vimto.

Maybe you are a hat.

Maybe you are a chair.

Maybe you are a soundbyte.

Maybe you are existing in a separate but simultaneous world
like when you were born you came out of a portal that was
surprisingly embedded in your mother's vagina and you
slithered into a slightly different world that looks like our world
but out of sync – ever so slightly underneath, subterranean or
slightly beside everyone else who agree on things and say all
together 'isn't that nice?' or 'isn't this important?' and your
mouth says 'yes yes' but you feel nothing and you search for
others like you and you collect them and they do not put their
eyeballs on you and think of untender sexual scenarios

And they are out there

And we are okay

(*Some moments*.)

(KES *emerges into view again*.)

Prison is prison.

It's not like *Orange is the New Black*, I'm sad to report. Much cry-ier. (Though we do all love that show, obviously.)

You don't get to speed off on a motorbike, people don't think you're a charming heartbreaker. It's scary for people who write headlines or become judges to think a girl would want to do those dude things.

I fucked up. Massive.

Won't go into the dark stuff about prison and stuff. No one likes a sad lesbian story, remember.

Let's skip that bit, okay? Yeah?

(KES *checks it is okay with us*.)

We appeal.

The appeal is successful. Press don't go so mad for that story.

Six months in prison. The conviction isn't overturned. But the sentence is. My heart starts to beat again. *Dut-dut, dut-dut, dut-dut* hello heart. Home. Bed. Doesn't fit me. Nothing kinda. Fits. The dog, he puts his dog-nose on me.

Don't feel evil.

Don't feel much. I'm on happy pills. Consider giving the dog one, but think better of it.

Eventually Dad makes a joke about me being the new Doctor Who, and I think maybe one day it might be okay again. Then the guy at the garage calls me a paedophile.

Comme ci comme ça.

Come back to the meet-up group.

(KES *faces us*.)

Doughnuts and Vimto at the break. Ha. Look down into my Vimto.

Didn't realise I could break laws. Hurt people. Hurt Jules. Least now I can put it in words. Want to help other people do that.

Lara's in the middle of complaining they should provide coconut water, suddenly hugs the air out of me – 'Cheer up, Kessy.'

No one's called me that in – . Not sure if I am. Kes.

Got a message from Jules.

Through her gamer avatar. She's finishing uni. Says she's confused, maybe bi. Says she's messed up. That um. I did that. Doesn't want me to contact her.

(*Soft*.) I know. I'm so. Sorry.

You nod. You *listen*.

I'm not naive any more. I'm older. I have words. There are more words now. In prison I was sent books. 'Gender binary.' 'Gender non-binary.' 'Agender.' I did those things. But they have played me like an avatar in someone else's game, the difficulty level on its highest setting so I'm telling it all to you myself so at least you might see me. I'm an okay human, I think. And so are you for listening. Can't speak for others, only myself. Flew close to a star. Dazzled myself. Fell backwards, scorched. Kes circled back to earth. People spoke loudly at me. The judge had grey hair and fresh flowers. My heart became a pixellated map, unable to pick out road signs let alone drop a pin so you could come and find me. It'll be a careful return.

Cos it's just as likely you are all aliens, and I am the earthling. There's just more of you.

Hands lifting me, taking the weight.

Life's too awesome not to – I'm, you know, really flippin –

(*Some moments*.)

Just so glad you guys are here. So.

Thanks.

Yeah, god, that's the short version, sorry!

Thanks.

My body bends like a bow, arrow pointed to the sun, exploding atoms

(*End.*)

A Nick Hern Book

Scorch first published in Great Britain in 2016 as a paperback original by
Nick Hern Books Limited, The Glasshouse, 49a Goldhawk Road, London W12 8QP,
in association with Prime Cut

Scorch copyright © 2016 Stacey Gregg

Stacey Gregg has asserted her moral right to be identified as the author of this
work

Cover image: Ben Willis at HiJump

Designed and typeset by Nick Hern Books, London
Printed in the UK by Mimeo Ltd, Huntingdon, Cambridgeshire PE29 6XX

A CIP catalogue record for this book is available from the British Library

ISBN 978 1 84842 612 2

www.nickhernbooks.co.uk

 facebook.com/nickhernbooks

twitter.com/nickhernbooks